DEDICATION AND MEMORIAL ADDRESS

By Chaplain William N. Thomas
United States Naval Academy
1945

★ ★ ★

Dedicated to the graduates of

the United States Naval Academy who have given

their lives in the line of duty while serving their country,

to all other military service members who have

faithfully served and to their families.

In remembrance of

_____

_____

TABLE OF CONTENTS

The Dedication
in Memorial Hall at the
United States Naval Academy
beneath the "Dont Give Up the Ship" Battle Flag

★ ★ ★

WITH IMMORTAL VALOR AND THE PRICE OF THEIR
LIVES THESE PROVED THEIR LOVE OF COUNTRY
AND THEIR LOYALTY TO THE HIGH TRADITIONS
OF THEIR ALMA MATER BY INSCRIBING WITH
THEIR OWN BLOOD THE NARRATIVE OF THEIR
DEEDS ABOVE, ON AND UNDERNEATH THE SEVEN
SEAS. THEY HAVE SET THE COURSE. THEY SILENTLY
STAND WATCH WHEREVER NAVY SHIPS PLY THE
WATERS OF THE GLOBE.

★ ★ ★

Chaplain William N. Thomas

Foreword

This memorial address was delivered by Chaplain Thomas on October 7, 1945, at the time of the United States Naval Academy's Centennial Celebration. Its inclusive spiritual statement embodies the important and sacred contributions made by the Naval Academy Graduates who gave their lives for their country.

The Address was printed in the Appendix to the United States Congressional Record dated October 18, 1945.

The
Creative Force
of the Great Dead

"So Elisha died and they buried him. Now bands of Moabites were in the habit of raiding the land at the coming in of the year. And while they were burying a man, suddenly they saw a marauding band. So they cast the man in the grave of Elisha and went on. But when the man touched the bones of Elisha, he revived and arose and stood on his feet." (II Kings 13: 20 and 21)

This strange story from the life of an ancient people is so remote from anything that we can conceive of as happening in our modern age that it may seem out of place in this service. Not only is the story told in the Bible but Josephus relates it in his writings. It probably belonged to the folk-lore of generations and was recited by the firesides of homes, in the market places of villages and towns, and carried by pilgrim bands across the boundaries of provinces and kingdoms.

Served Six Kings

Elisha was a great man. He served at the court of six succeeding kings. The enemies of his country feared him. When they were tempted to invade the land, they thought of Elisha and changed their plans. It was said that he was worth more than a thousand generals. The people felt secure as long as Elisha was near. Then, the day came when the great patriot of indomitable spirit died.

But alien armies were still afraid of the land in which his body was buried, and his countrymen still believed that his spirit protected them. So, the story was told to friend and stranger of how a man who was dead touched the bones of Elisha, was revived, arose, and stood on his feet. It was their homely way of expressing a great truth which the centuries have affirmed—*The Creative Force of the Great Dead.*

The Creative Force of the Great Dead

No subject could be more appropriate for this day when we gather in these sacred walls to pay grateful tribute to the graduates of this academy who, during the century of its existence, have given their lives in the service of their country. Yet, we cannot help but approach this hour, set apart from all the hours of a century, and dedicated to lives that are particularly sacred to us, with mixed emotions of sorrow and joy, humility and pride, and a consuming sense of inadequacy.

Quotes Lincoln

Other schools hold memorial services for their graduates – graduates who have gone out from the school. But, these belong to our firesides. They are fathers and husbands, friends and brothers–and sons. Their sacrifices make every inch of these grounds, on which they once walked, hallowed earth. Their glory is beyond the poverty of our language. In the words of Abraham Lincoln at Gettysburg, "It is beyond my poor power to add or detract. The world will little note nor long remember what we say here, but it will never forget what they did."

The world does not forget what the great dead have done. Theirs is a creative force that revives, leads, and inspires. Without them history would be as monotonous as the march of trading caravans across the desert. Therefore, they live. They must live because they silently reveal to us the creative elements of human character that defy circumstances and conditions, and grow more lustrous with the passing of the centuries.

The great dead live because their lives embody imperishable and indestructible components of life that are indispensable in the upward march of the race.

Creative Force of Their Ideals

In the first place, they are alive in the *Creative Force of Their Ideals.* A French nobleman and philanthropist (La Rochefoucauld) of the 18th century wrote the first rule of greatness when he said, "Great souls are not those who have fewer passions and more virtues than the common lot, but those only who have greater designs." As Lowell expressed it, "To have greatly dreamed precludes low ends."

Aims Were Great

As we mark the deeds of the great dead we soon discover that their deeds are great because their aims were great. Their ideals are the woof of their work. As these ideals are tested by a century of loyalty through alternating peace and war, they gather the allegiance of succeeding generations till they are moulded into high tradition, the legacy of the great dead.

Nothing is more real than the power of this intangible force. The difference in the value and the influence of the Naval Academy of 1945 and the school that opened its doors here one hundred years ago is not primarily the difference in material equipment. It is the difference made by men who have provided, whatever the cost, the excellency of its purpose. And indeed, as we are the inheritors of their designs, they, in their day, built on the great purposes of those who lived before them.

Creative Force of Unselfish Action

Silent Teachers

In the classrooms of October 1845 there were silent teachers–
Jones, Lawrence, Perry, Decatur. That they have never been
absent, since that beginning is written in the records of the
century's heroic dead. One hundred and thirty years after James
Lawrence, dying of battle wounds, set the standard with his
famous words, "Don't give up the ship," that standard was re-
echoed by Howard Gilmore, as he lay mortally wounded on the
bridge of his submarine, "Take her down."

The spirit of these and countless others is appropriately inscribed
on the bronze doors of this chapel – *Non sibi sed patriae* – Not for
self but for country. The creative force of the great dead lingers
through the motives by which they lived and for which they died.

In the second place, the graduates of the Academy who have
given their lives in the service of their country live in the *Creative
Force of Unselfish Action.* High resolves may be expressed in the
eloquence of language: great living can only be expressed in great
deeds. In the words of Lord Lytton, "That man is great, and he
alone, who serves a greatness not his own."

Measured by this exacting yard-stick those on the role of honor
of this institution demand a "Well done." We would not paint
them in saints' garments who like Francis of Assisi exchanged all
their desires and possessions for penance and beggars' rags. They
were too human for that. But, they met Shakespeare's challenge,
"Be great in act as you have been in thought." Like saints, they
proved their faith by their works.

Unique Nobility

On the Walls

On the walls of this chapel are two examples of a unique nobility—the nobility of first place. The inscriptions on two plaques are strikingly similar. One reads, "Bagley, the first American officer who fell in the Spanish-American war." The other reads, "Thomas, the first officer of any of the armed forces of the United States to lose his life in conflict in the World War." Would that we could call all the names of those who have exemplified Henry Ward Beecher's lines, "Greatness lies not in being strong but in the right use of strength."

It is fitting that they should be honored in this house of prayer in the dedication of the window of The Commission Invisible: "In reverent tribute to all the sons of their Alma Mater who in war and peace have realized her ideals of honor, courage, loyalty and duty in the service of God and country this window is placed here."

Creative Force of Their Dying

Creative Power

We have mentioned the creative force of the ideals and the unselfish actions of the Academy's honored dead. There is still another, the *Creative Force of Their Dying* – the creative power of the supreme sacrifice. Isaac Kidd, and many after him in the war now about to fade into history, made it silently. On the base of this beautifully carved pulpit are two significant words–An Appreciation, A Memorial – and many of you think of Chandler's last words on the bridge of his ship were, "This is the price we pay." It is the price they all paid – the price of their ideals and their unselfish service. It is also a never-dying inheritance bequeathed by them to their school, their Navy, and their country.

As the figure of the Christ stands on the waters of the sea, in the window back of the altar, that symbolizes our faith in the God of goodness and justice, we dare to believe that this Man of Galilee, so perfect in ideals, unselfish service, and great dying, accepts the companionship of our beloved dead who followed him in proportion to their knowledge and strength.

Young Graduates

You will forgive me if I close with a special reference to the young graduates who in the past four years have proved their right to wear the blue and gold. Time has not yet written their names among yesterday's great. In the language of Sala, they are "Heroes without the laurel and conquerors without the triumph." They went from these peaceful walls to the terrors of war, with their uniforms new and their insignia bright. With thousands of other young men "theirs to do and to die." (Tennyson) They did both in keeping with the century of traditions behind them. Russell Davenport in his great book, "My Country," writes of an immortality that belongs to them.

On the shore where the stiff white crosses work a design for eternity,

And the lives of men are but numbers, and an alien wind

Comes up to the beaches, caressing

The fallen sons of a distant country;

Here, at last the meaning of truth and freedom

Opens, unsealed, before the eyes of the nations;

Where death has merged the memories of Maine and Nebraska,

Of Indian fires in the desert, of bearded live oaks,

The motion of Texas grass when the wind is moving,

The dusty roads that lead to schools and churches.

Here they merge like a stream–branches and orchards,

Court houses, banks, shops, railroads, and factories,

Memories of faces, of lips parted with passion,

Of hands like sunlight on the nerves, of hair fallen

Over the shoulders of someone beyond the ocean.

Here in the name of freedom all have gathered

Into the perfect union of purposes united–

A brotherhood of men in the arms of death.

Open these graves to discover.

The secret of liberty shoveled under the earth;

The boys to our hearts, like shadows of ourselves;

To re-inhabit the land where they cannot live.

Who are with her no more in the shape of their hands and their faces.

But are in us forever a part of her being;

Let us live therefore, in the name of those who have fallen,

That in our lives they may be resurrected;

Let us search for the light by which to find them

Within ourselves and in one another...

Let us uncover the graves...

Let us pray...

Almighty God, our Father, in whose holy keeping are the living and the dead; we thank Thee for the valor of those who have gone down to the sea in ships, for the glory of their deeds on the great waters, and for the everlasting benefits of their sacrifices. Help us to so live that we shall have a right to claim the noble franchise they have left us–through Jesus Christ our Lord.

Benediction

O Lord God, when Thou givest to Thy servants
to endeavor any great matter, grant us also to know that it
is not the beginning, but the continuing of the same until
it is thoroughly finished, which yieldeth the true glory;
through Him that for the finishing
of Thy work, laid down His life, our Redeemer,
Jesus Christ. Amen.

★ ★ ★

Midshipman Prayer

Almighty Father, whose way is in the sea, and whose paths are in the great waters, whose command is over all and whose love never faileth: Let me be aware of Thy presence and obedient to Thy will. Keep me true to my best self, guarding me against dishonesty in purpose and in deed, and helping me so to live that I can stand unashamed and unafraid before my shipmates, my loved ones, and Thee. Protect those in whose love I live. Give me the will to do the work of a man and to accept my share of responsibilities with a strong heart and a cheerful mind. Make me considerate of those entrusted to my leadership and faithful to the duties my country has entrusted to me. Let my uniform remind me daily of the traditions of the service of which I am a part. If I am inclined to doubt, steady my faith; if I am tempted, make me strong to resist; if I should miss the mark, give me courage to try again. Guide me with the light of truth and keep before me the life of Him by whose example and help I trust to obtain the answer to my prayer, Jesus Christ our Lord. Amen.

Midshipman Prayer
Interfaith Version

Almighty God, whose way is in the sea, whose paths are in the great waters, whose command is over all and whose love never faileth; let me be aware of Thy presence and obedient to Thy will. Keep me true to my best self, guarding me against dishonesty in purpose and in deed, and helping me so to live that I can stand unashamed and unafraid before my shipmates, my loved ones, and Thee. Protect those in whose love I live. Give me the will to do my best and to accept my share of responsibilities with a strong heart and a cheerful mind. Make me considerate of those entrusted to my leadership and faithful to the duties my country has entrusted in me. Let my uniform remind me daily of the traditions of the service of which I am a part. If I am inclined to doubt, steady my faith; if I am tempted, make me strong to resist; if I should miss the mark, give me courage to try again. Guide me with the light of truth and give me strength to faithfully serve thee, now and always. Amen.

The Navy Hymn
Eternal Father, Strong to Save

Eternal Father strong to save,
Whose arm hath bound the restless
wave,
Who bid'st the mighty ocean deep
Its own appointed limits keep;
Oh hear us when we cry to Thee,
For those in peril on the sea!

O Christ! Whose voice the waters heard
And hushed their raging at Thy word,
Who walked'st on the foaming deep,
And calm amidst its rage didst sleep;
Oh, hear us when we cry to Thee,
For those in peril on the sea!

Most Holy Spirit! Who didst brood
Upon the chaos dark and rude,
And bid its angry tumult cease,
And give, for wild confusion, peace;
Oh, hear us when we cry to Thee,
For those in peril on the sea!

Eternal Father, grant, we pray,
To all Marines, both night and day,
The courage, honor, strength, and skill
Their land to serve, thy law fulfill;
Be thou the shield forevermore
From every peril to the Corps!

Lord, guard and guide all those who fly
Through the great spaces in the sky.
Be with them always in the air,
In darkening storms or sunlight fair;
Oh, hear us when we lift our prayer,
For those in peril in the air!

Lord God, our power evermore,
Whose arm doth reach the ocean floor,
Dive with brave beneath the sea;
Traverse the depths protectively.
O hear us when we pray, and keep
Them safe from perils in the deep!

O Trinity of love and power!
Our brethren shield in danger's hour;
From rock and tempest, fire and foe,
Protect them wheresoe'er they go;
Thus evermore shall rise to Thee,
Glad hymns of praise from land and sea.

Adapted from the Original
Words by William Whiting
Music by John B. Dykes
1860-1861

★ ★ ★

Addendum

Bancroft Hall

Bancroft Hall (1908) is the largest building at the United States Naval Academy and the largest single dormitory in the world. It was named after former United States Secretary of the Navy, historian and statesman George Bancroft (1800-1891) who founded the Academy in 1845. The hall is home for the entire brigade of approximately 4,000 midshipmen. It is referred to as "Mother B" or "The Hall". It contains many support services, stores, clinics and the dining hall, King Hall, where all eat simultaneously. It is named for Fleet Admiral Ernest King (1878-1956) who was Chief of Naval Operations and Commander in Chief of the U.S. Fleet in the Second World War.

Memorial Hall opens off the central Rotunda up the grand staircase. The hall contains the honor roll of more than 2,600 Naval Academy alumni who have died in combat or military operations and who are listed on the walls. There are other memorials, plaques and paintings of ships and sea battles in the hall.

The Dedication in Memorial Hall below the Dont Give Up the Ship flag was written by RADM William Nathaniel Thomas (1892-1971), Chaplain, USN who was the Seventh US Navy Chief of Chaplains (1945-1949). The USNA Virtual Memorial Hall was created and is maintained by the Run to Honor organization which provides a listing and the history of the honorees on the internet.

★ ★ ★

RADM, William N. Thomas, CHC, USN

William Nathaniel Thomas was born in 1892 and was from Piney Woods, Mississippi. He was one fourth Choctaw Indian. Chaplain Thomas got his preacher's license when he was 16. He graduated from Millsaps College and Seashore Divinity School. Joining the First World War effort, the Army had no need for chaplains, so he enlisted in the Navy never having seen a naval officer.

As a Navy chaplain, he made twenty-eight trips with troops across the Atlantic in 1918-19 serving onboard the *USS Madawaska*. He then served onboard the *USS Pennsylvania* in

1923-24. In 1928-29 he was the chaplain aboard the *USS Raleigh* for a State Department goodwill tour to Europe and the Middle East. He then served on the *USS West Virginia* in 1932-33.

Chaplain Thomas had a tour of duty at the United States Naval Academy in Annapolis from 1924-27 as an Assistant Chaplain and returned as Command Chaplain from 1933-45 – the longest tenure of a Naval Academy chaplain. He wrote *The Prayer of a Midshipman* in 1938. Chaplain Thomas oversaw the expansion of the Chapel extending the nave with its anchors, votive ship and pulpit, dedicating it in 1941. Chaplain Thomas was also instrumental in bringing Jewish clergy to the Academy.

Chief of Chaplains from 1945 until 1949, he oversaw the demobilization of 2,800 chaplains at the end the Second World War and revised the Chaplain Corps. He was the first chaplain to be promoted to Rear Admiral, upper-half, permanent status. He was awarded the Legion of Merit.

Chaplain Thomas wrote the Dedication in Memorial Hall at the Academy. The walk encircling the Academy Chapel is named in his honor. He retired after 33 years of service in 1949.

★ ★ ★

Biographical Glossary

Saint Francis of Assisi, c.1181-1226 An Italian Roman Catholic friar, deacon, and preacher, and one of the most venerated religious figures in history.

Worth Bagley, 1874-1898 An ensign and the only U.S. Navy officer killed in action during the Spanish-American War.

Henry Ward Beecher, 1813-1887 A Congregationalist preacher who emphasized God's love and was also known for his support for the abolition of slavery.

Theodore Edson Chandler, 1894-1945 U.S. Naval Academy class of 1915. A Rear Admiral in the U.S. Navy during World War II who was killed in action by a Japanese kamikaze strike aboard the flag ship, *USS Louisville*.

Jesus Christ, Man from Galilee, Jesus of Nazareth, c. 4 B.C.-c. 30/33 A.D. A preacher and religious figure. In Christianity he is believed to be the Messiah.

Russell Wheeler Davenport, 1899-1954 An American writer and publisher who served with the army in World War I. Known for his 1944 poem "My Country, a Poem of America."

Stephen Decatur, Jr., 1779-1820 A naval officer who played a significant role in the early development of the U.S. Navy. He became the first post-Revolutionary War hero for his naval accomplishments.

Howard Walter Gilmore, 1902-1943 A submarine commander in the U.S. Navy during World War II who sacrificed himself with the command "Take her down!" aboard the submarine *USS Growler* when he was unable to escape below. He received the Medal of Honor posthumously.

John Paul Jones, 1747-1792 An immigrant from Scotland. He was a hero of the United States Navy and a Commander in the American Revolutionary War. He is buried in the crypt of the Naval Academy Chapel in Annapolis, Maryland.

Isaac Campbell Kidd, 1884-1941 A Rear Admiral in the United States Navy. He was killed on the bridge of *USS Arizona* during the Japanese attack on Pearl Harbor.

François de La Rochefoucauld, Prince de Marcillac, 1613-1680 A noted French author of maxims and memoirs.

Capt. James Lawrence, 1781-1813 A U.S. naval captain best known for his last words, "Dont give up the ship!" which his friend Oliver Hazard Perry put on his personal battle flag to commemorate Lawrence's death.

Abraham Lincoln, 1809-1865 The 16th President of the United States during the Civil War years. He was assassinated while attending a play at Ford's Theatre, Washington, D.C. in 1865.

Robert Trail Spence Lowell, IV, 1917-1977 A noted American poet who won many awards for his work.

Robert Bulwer-Lytton, First Earl of Lytton, 1831-1891 An English poet and statesman, as well as an accomplished and popular diplomat.

Oliver Hazard Perry, 1785-1819 A U.S. naval commander, remembered for his personal battle flag which he emblazoned with "Dont give up the ship!" to commemorate Captain Lawrence's last words.

George Augustus Henry Sala, 1828-1895 An English journalist known for his words, "Heroes without the laurel, and conquerors without the triumph."

William Shakespeare, 1564 -1616 An English playwright, popularly thought to be one of the greatest writers and dramatists of all time.

Alfred, Lord Tennyson, 1809-1892 Poet Laureate of Great Britain and Ireland from 1850 until his death in 1892. He was one of England's best known poets.

Lt. Clarence Crase Thomas, 1886-1917 U.S. Naval Academy Class of 1910. The first naval officer to die in World War I. He was posthumously awarded the Navy Cross.

★ ★ ★

Significant Organizations

United States Navy
United States Navy Chaplains Corps
Chief of Chaplains of the United States Navy
Navy Chaplaincy Center and School

United States Naval Academy
USNA Chaplains Center
USNA Alumni Association and Foundation
Honor Our Fallen Heroes
Run To Honor

Wikipedias
William Nathaniel Thomas, RADM, CHC, USN
Prayer of a Midshipman
Bancroft Hall - Dedication
Many of those individuals quoted in this Address

Book Creator
Richard K. Templeton, M.D.
Annapolis, Maryland
templetonrk@gmail.com

Note from Richard K. Templeton, M.D.
Grandson of Chaplain Thomas

When I first read Chaplain Thomas' address, I thought it celebrated the United States Naval Academy Centennial, but was struck to read this most sacred and powerful message to the Academy's Graduates whose lives were sacrificed for their country. I felt that this message should be shared and made available to the families of our fallen heroes and all others.

Richard K. Templeton, M.D.
Annapolis, MD 21401
templetonrk@gmail.com

Copies and electronic versions are available through book retailers worldwide.

★ ★ ★

www.ingramcontent.com/pod-product-compliance
Lightning Source LLC
Chambersburg PA
CBHW041959090426

42811CB00030B/1954/J